CHAPTER 1
Not Just a Regular Kid

From the start, Mr and Mrs Q knew that their baby daughter was smart. After all, it's not every day that you see a baby doing the family accounts.

But Betty Q was more than smart. She was like a walking computer in ballet slippers.

3

"Betty, what's a six letter word
meaning one and only?"asked Dad.
"Unique," chirped Betty.

"Your new invention works
like a charm," Mum said.
"Just something I've been playing around
with," said Betty.

rman

Illustrated by Maddy McClellan

W

FRANKLIN WATTS

Of course, once word got out, things got pretty busy around the Q residence. Everyone wanted Betty Q's help and the doorbell didn't stop ringing!

Ding Dong!

"We're here to recruit Betty," said a government official.

Ding Dong!

"Ever considered the space

programme, Betty?"

Ding Dong!

"Who is it, Betty?" asked Mum.

"No one important,"

answered Betty.

Nevertheless Betty Q turned them all down.
She just wanted to be a regular kid and do
regular kid things.

But in Betty's hometown of Dullville,

regular things never seemed to happen.

CHAPTER 2
The Cupcake Conundrum

At school one Friday morning Miss Marshall discovered that Molly's birthday cupcakes were missing. Cupcakes were sure to be a big hit in the classroom, but when Miss Marshall opened the box, all that was left were crumbs!

Immediately the children started
to blame each other.

"It was Reggie," accused Jenny.

"He's always wanting more food."

"It was Jenny," shouted Reggie.

"She likes anything the colour pink."

Miss Marshall explained that Molly's dad had dropped off the cupcakes the night before. The cupcakes went missing before anyone had arrived at school.

"They must have been stolen last night," said Reggie. "The school was burgled!"

Soon Principal Pio arrived to see what all the fuss was about. He confirmed that nothing else was missing and all the windows and doors were intact.

"The school was not burgled," he said.

"Then someone must have had a key," pointed out Shannon. "But who has a key to the school?"

The children considered the suspects.

"Caretakers have keys," said Jenny.
Caretaker Smith suddenly looked very uncomfortable.

"It wasn't me! I wasn't even here last night," explained Caretaker Smith.

"Look, the bins are still full."

"A likely story," huffed Reggie.

"It's true," continued Caretaker Smith.

"I was at the Big Bingo tournament and I won."

Caretaker Smith's alibi was pretty good.

By now, everyone was at a loss.

"What a conundrum," said Principal Pio.

"Maybe Miss Marshall forgot to put the cupcakes in the box," said Reggie.

"Maybe the cupcakes just disappeared," suggested Shannon.

"Maybe there's a ghost," squeaked Billy.

"I have the answer," said Betty Q.

CHAPTER 3
The Culprit Revealed

As always, Betty Q was doing two very
important things that she always did:
listening and observing. She walked very
slowly around the room, got out her spy
glass and began…

"I know who stole the cupcakes and the thief is here in this room."

Now Betty had everyone's attention.

"Let's review the facts," she continued.

"One: Miss Marshall put the cupcakes on the highest shelf, so the thief had to reach up high."

"That's true," said Miss Marshall. "I put the cupcakes on the "Very Important Things' shelf, for safe keeping."

"Two: I noticed crumbs on the floor.

The thief must have eaten the cupcakes

inside the classroom."

"So the thief had to be able to reach up high

and have access to the classroom,"

deduced Jenny.

"Oh my goodness children, don't look at me!" exclaimed Principal Pio.

"It wasn't Principal Pio," said Betty Q.

"But you said the thief had to reach the top shelf," complained Jack. "Only someone who is tall could do that."

"And you said the thief ate the cupcakes inside the classroom," said Shannon.

"Who else could get in without a key?"

"You don't have to get inside the classroom if you've never left," Betty said. "And you don't have to be tall if you can…fly! Fact three: probably the most important evidence of all, the thief did not finish eating the cupcakes."

"Here's your thief!"
announced Betty Q.
"Jo-Jo!" cried
the children.

"But what about the cupcakes?" sniffed

Molly. "We won't have any for my party."

"Don't worry," said Miss Marshall.

"Luckily there are plenty of treats left

Jo-Jo hasn't been able to eat."

"Mystery solved thanks to Betty,"
said Principal Pio, congratulating her.
But cupcakes weren't the only thing to go
missing in Dullville that day. Betty was
about to get her biggest case yet.

"Betty, come quickly!" Wendy called.

"Patty Packer's pet shop has just
been robbed!"

CHAPTER 4
The Disappearing Dog

Betty Q and her friends ran to Patty

Packer's Pet Shop and found her pouting

on the porch.

"It's a disaster," she wailed. "My perfect

poodle, Snowflake, has been stolen!"

Patty's prized pooch was supposed to compete in the Dullville Pet Show later that afternoon, but when Patty returned to pick up Snowflake from the shop, she was gone.

"Minny, my shopkeeper, said there were only three people in the shop today," said Patty. Then she walked over to a pen full of poodles and added some biscuits to their bowl. A group of black poodles raced over. "Snowflake would have won first prize today for sure," sniffed Patty.

"Would you mind if we talked to Minny?"

Betty asked. Minny was by the shelves,

stacking tins of dog food.

"How do we know Minny didn't take

Snowflake?" asked Reggie.

"I would never hurt Snowflake," Minny

gasped. "I put Snowflake in the poodle pen

with the other dogs this morning. I fed the

dogs at noon and Snowflake was still there."

"But when I got here at two o'clock, Snowflake was missing," said Patty.

"Who else was in the shop?" asked Jenny.

"There was one customer who bought a kitten this morning," said Minny. "And in the afternoon, another customer bought a lizard. At the same time, a delivery person dropped off fresh cut flowers."

"I bet it was the lizard customer,"
said Shannon. "After all, who buys a lizard
as a pet anyway?"

Minny shook her head. "I was with him the
whole time. He did not steal Snowflake."

"Maybe someone came into the shop
without you knowing," offered Reggie.

"We keep the doors locked so that no
animals get out," said Patty. "Everyone must
be let in and out of the shop with a key."

"May we walk around?" asked Betty Q.
As always, Betty Q was doing two very
important things that she always did:
listening and observing.

"It's as if Snowflake vanished into thin air," whined Patty.

Betty got out her spy glass and began.

"I know exactly where Snowflake is."

CHAPTER 5
Mystery Solved!

Now Betty had everyone's attention.

"Let's review the facts," she began.

"There is only one door to the shop,"

said Betty. "And that door is locked except

for when Minny opens it with a key."

"Right, I only opened and closed it three times," Minny confirmed. "And no one left with Snowflake."

"After the kitten customer left this morning, Snowflake was still in her pen," said Betty. "Correct," confirmed Minny.

"And you were with the lizard customer the whole time," said Betty.

"Correct," confirmed Minny.

"Of course if you were busy with the lizard customer, then you couldn't have been watching the flower delivery man," deduced Betty.

"But he just dropped off flowers," said Minny. "And when I let him out of the shop, he didn't have Snowflake."

Betty walked over to the flowers on the counter. "You said that the man delivered fresh cut flowers," said Betty.

"Yes, we get them every week," said Patty.

Betty took out one of the flowers and held it up to Patty's nose.

"What do you smell?" asked Betty.

"I can't smell anything," said Patty.

"That's right," said Betty. "Because these flowers are fake."

"But why would someone deliver fake fresh cut flowers?" asked Reggie.

"Because someone wanted to use the vase to hold something else instead of water," said Betty. Then Betty emptied the vase. Out popped a bottle of black paint.

"What is the paint for?" asked Jenny.

Betty walked over to the poodle pen and picked up one of the dogs. She took it to the dog bath and ran the water.

"To paint a white poodle black," said Betty, turning around to reveal a white poodle.

"Snowflake!" everyone yelled.

"While Minny was distracted with the customer looking for a lizard, the flower delivery man painted the only white dog in the shop black to match the other poodles."

"Oh thank you, Betty," said Patty holding Snowflake tight. "I bet that wasn't a real delivery man. It was probably Mr Barker. His parrot is competing in the pet show today as well."

"Well there's still time to clean up Snowflake for the competition," said Betty. "Good luck!"

"Good work, Betty, another case solved," Billy said as Betty and her friends walked back to school.

"And to think Mr Barker almost got away with his evil plan. Without Snowflake competing, Mr Barker's parrot would have won the Dullville Pet Show for sure."

"Oh I doubt that," Betty said with a smile. "Mr Barker's pet can sing but it's hard for a parrot to sing with a stomach ache or should I say cupcake ache."

"You mean...?" Jenny gasped.

Betty Q nodded. "Jo-Jo is Mr Barker's pet parrot. Mr Barker lent him to the school for National Pet Week. But while he was busy scheming, his parrot was eating too many cupcakes!"

"It serves Mr Barker right," giggled Molly. "Speaking of cupcakes, can we have my party now?"

"Of course," said Betty. "Hopefully the rest of our day will be nothing but...regular."

43

Of course in Betty's hometown of Dullville, regular things never seemed to happen...

"Betty, come quick!"

They *still try to* recruit her

for government services.

They *still* beg her to join

the space programme.

And they *still* consult her on important issues (which we still can't talk about.)

But Betty Q has her hands full...

...just being a kid.

First published in 2014 by
Franklin Watts
338 Euston Road
London
NW1 3BH

Franklin Watts Australia
Level 17/207 Kent Street
Sydney
NSW 2000

Text © Karyn Gorman 2014
Illustration © Maddy McClellan 2014

The rights of Karyn Gorman to be
identified as the author and Maddy
McClellan as the illustrator of this Work
have been asserted in accordance with the
Copyright, Designs and Patents Act, 1988.

Series Editor: Melanie Palmer
Series Advisor: Catherine Glavina
Series Designer: Cathryn Gilbert

A CIP catalogue record for this book is
available from the British Library.

ISBN 978 1 4451 3361 4 (hbk)
ISBN 978 1 4451 3362 1 (pbk)
ISBN 978 1 4451 3364 5 (ebook)
ISBN 978 1 4451 3363 8 (library ebook)

Printed in China

Franklin Watts is a division of Hachette
Children's Books, an Hachette UK company.
www.hachette.co.uk